The New Jim Crow
Study Guide and
Call to Action

The Veterans of Hope Project

The New Jim Crow Study Guide and Call to Action

The Veterans of Hope Project is a multifaceted educational initiative on religion, culture, and participatory democracy. We encourage a healing-centered approach to community-building that recognizes the interconnectedness of spirit, creativity, and citizenship. Our educational materials are designed to support reconciliation, nonviolence, and an appreciation for the value of indigenous and folk wisdom for contemporary times.

The New Jim Crow Study Guide and Call to Action grew out of conversations among Chris Moore-Backman, Vincent Harding, and Michelle Alexander over the course of 2012. Special thanks to photographers Richard Ross, Lloyd DeGrane, Julia Rendleman, Bob Fitch, and Jon Lowenstein for permission to use their work.

Page citations for *The New Jim Crow* correspond with the 2012 paperback edition (also available as an e-book).

Design and composition by Bookbright Media.

Copies of this booklet are available to groups free of charge at: www.NewJimCrowOrganizing.org

Photo © Bob Fitch—www.bobfitchphoto.com

In honor of Martin Luther King Jr. and the movement that raised him up as spokesperson.

CONTENTS

FOREWORD

Vincent Harding, Chairperson, the Veterans of Hope Project

For those of us who have begun to discover the extraordinary experience of Michelle Alexander's wise and compassionate work, *The New Jim Crow*, for those of us who wish to enter more fully into the book's amazing richness, this Study Guide and Call to Action is a great gift and a powerful challenge.

It is a gift because it opens the way for us—individually and collectively—to explore the message of *The New Jim Crow* even more deeply than we might have been able to without such thoughtful guidance and provocative stimulation. At the same time, this Guide is also an urgent invitation to transformation. For it insists that we take seriously Professor Alexander's demanding call not simply to read and understand her words, but to hear as well the voice of Martin Luther King Jr. and his countless comrades in struggle, calling to his country, their country, our country, "America, you must be born again." This Study Guide reminds us that Alexander takes King deeply into her heart, and with him she encourages us to do the demanding work of creating "a more perfect union"—a country free from the dehumanizing scourge of mass incarceration.

Of course, the Study Guide and Call to Action also challenges us to recognize how much we need each other's accompaniment for the work at hand: studying, exploring, imagining together, we will likely discover the wisdom of an African-American elder who recently wrote, "The American experiment [with multi-racial democracy] is still in the laboratory." And sister Michelle—along with the Guide and the Call—reminds us that we create the Beloved Community as we work together on the continuing, daunting task.

In case we have any questions about precisely who is meant to do the work in the laboratory, the late June Jordan, beloved co-worker and poet, would add her loving wisdom to the call of Michelle, the call of King, of Ella Baker, of Fannie Lou Hamer and Anne Braden, the call of all the black and brown young people who are locked away from our sight: "We are the ones we've been waiting for." Working with the Guide we hear the call: We are the ones who must not allow anyone—especially anyone young, filled with color and in need of a new life—to be locked away from our sight, from our heart.

We are the ones that our children (and aren't they all our children?) behind bars, behind fears, behind hopelessness, are waiting for. We are the ones this nation, our nation, is waiting for. Let's continue the great experiment in great hope, moving relentlessly forward toward a more perfect union, sharing our hope with all the imprisoned sons and daughters, sisters and brothers, fathers and mothers, building the Beloved Community as we go. Responding to the call to action that begins deep within us, we discover a new freedom for our children, a new freedom for our nation and for ourselves. We discover Langston Hughes's great complaint and great commitment:

O, yes,
I say it plain,
America never was America to me,
And yet I swear this oath—
America will be!

This is the gift and the challenge to which the Guide points us. Are we ready to hear the call? Are we ready to hunger and thirst? Are we ready to be filled?

USING THIS GUIDE

We hope that *The New Jim Crow Study Guide and Call to Action* will be used by a great many groups meeting in a wide variety of settings. The guide has been organized accordingly as a very flexible document, leaving room for each group to discover its own style for engaging with the material. It begins with an introduction followed by four main sections. These sections share a simple three-part format: an opening quotation from *The New Jim Crow*, a narrative section, and a series of discussion topics and questions.

The guide covers a lot of ground. Depending on your group's interests and circumstances, you may choose to cover all of the material, or you may opt to hone in on particular topics. Whatever the case, as you enter your work together, we encourage you and support you in striving for a group experience that is inclusive, democratic, and emotionally safe for all participants. Toward this end, as your process develops, we think it will be essential to invite and open up the gifts and resources of each person in your group, and to trust that everyone has something of deep value to offer.

In addition to exploring and grappling with the content in the guide, we hope you will protect time and space to reflect together on your group's process. It will be up to you to name what is working and what is not working in your sessions together and to make the needed adjustments. This type of reflection and recalibration takes time. What's more—as is the case with just about everything folks work on together—it will undoubtedly call for "the 3 C's" that were so characteristic of Martin Luther King's approach to social change organizing, and to life in general: Courage to see, speak, and hear the truth; Creativity to chart the needed, often unseen course; and Compassion for ourselves and our companions along the way.

Photo © Richard Ross—juvenile-in-justice.com

INTRODUCTION

I want to discuss the race problem tonight and I want
to discuss it very honestly. I still believe that freedom
is the bonus you receive for telling the truth. "Ye shall
know the truth and the truth shall set you free." And
I do not see how we will ever solve the turbulent
problem of race confronting our nation until there is
an honest confrontation with it and a willing search for
the truth and a willingness to admit the truth when we
discover it.

—Martin Luther King Jr., March 14, 1968

Now and then a book comes along that sounds an
alarm, challenging prevailing ways of viewing and in-
terpreting our world and exposing a profound injustice that
is hidden in plain sight. *The New Jim Crow* is such a book.
But it is more than that. It is a call to conscience, a call to
action. The book argues that nothing short of a major social
movement—a human rights movement rooted in the recog-
nition of the basic dignity and humanity of all of us—holds

any hope for ending mass incarceration and breaking the cycle of caste in the United States.

This call to conscience and action has struck a chord nationwide, across lines of race, class, ethnicity, and religion. Many were stunned when the paperback version of the book shot to the *New York Times* bestseller list and stayed there, month after month. After all, this is the age of Obama—a time when discussions of racism and systems of racial control are supposed to be part of our nation's history, not our present. Yet the book boldly challenges the standard rhetoric and narrative about race in this country, and calls for a new multi-racial, multi-ethnic human rights movement, one that builds upon the contributions and sacrifices of abolitionists, freedom fighters, and civil rights advocates who labored to make the United States what it must become. The call has echoed both inside and outside the walls of prisons and jails. Its core message has been embraced by the young and the old, and by people from all walks of life. Law school students, seminary students, college students and high school students have pored over the pages, discussing and debating its content and implications. Faith-based study circles have been formed in places of worship nationwide. Book clubs of all types and stripes have found that the book has stimulated discussions like none other had before. Behind prison walls the book has been passed from cell to cell, and in drug treatment centers and mental health conferences professionals who aim to serve those who are struggling to survive "on the outside" have used the book to train counselors and advocates about the parallel social universe that exists for those labeled criminals.

This guide is meant to assist all those who are willing to do what has become nearly taboo in America: engage in deep and meaningful dialogue about race, racism, and structural inequality. It raises critical questions about how we—individually and collectively—view and treat those who find themselves cycling in and out of our nation's prisons and jails. Most importantly, this guide is meant to encourage readers to go beyond the four corners of the book and consider what is required of us at this moment in our nation's history. What would it mean for us to answer *The New Jim Crow*'s call for movement-building in our own schools, places of worship, neighborhoods, prisons, and reentry centers? What does the book have to say to us about the living of our own lives?

In order to answer such questions in any meaningful way, we must first be willing to do what Dr. King urged us to do decades ago: engage in a willing search for the truth and admit the truth when we discover it. This guide is meant to facilitate open and honest reflection about how we got here—how we managed to create, nearly overnight, a penal system unprecedented in world history that is filled largely with poor people of color, even as millions here at home and around the world imagine that we have "transcended" race with the election of President Barack Obama. We must discuss and debate how the system of mass incarceration actually works (as opposed to how it is advertised) so that our discussions about how best to respond can be grounded in fact, not popular myth. And last, but not least, "We the People" must be willing to search for the truth—and admit the truth—about ourselves, our own biases, stereotypes, and misconceptions, and the ways in which we might actually be part of the problem. If we muster the courage to face the truth about ourselves, our history, and our present, we have reason to hope for a radically better future.

We hope that the conversations catalyzed by *The New Jim Crow* and supported by this guide will lead to concerted action to address one of the most extraordinary human rights crises of our time. As noted in the foreword by Dr. Vincent Harding, the guide draws generously from the words and thought of Martin Luther King Jr. Dr. King's writings and speeches characteristically interweave the spiritual, the social, and the political, and his observations about the role of race in the United States remain searingly relevant in this era of mass incarceration. His insights remind us that our current struggle is part of a very old, very long struggle—a river of resistance and creative, collective action—to which King and countless other courageous souls gave their time, energy, love, and in some cases their very lives. As we move forward together, may the knowledge that we are part of that lineage ground us and inspire us.

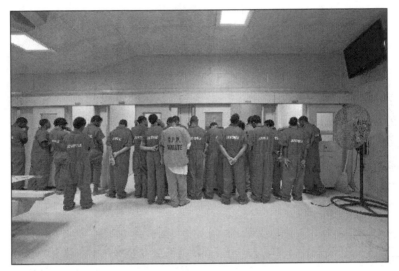

Photo © Richard Ross—juvenile-in-justice.com

SECTION ONE:
THE RECURRING CYCLE

(Introduction and Chapter One of The New Jim Crow)

The fate of millions of people—indeed the future of the black community itself—may depend on the willingness of those who care about racial justice to re-examine their basic assumptions about the role of the criminal justice system in our society. The fact that more than half of the young black men in many large American cities are currently under the control of the criminal justice system (or saddled with criminal records) is not—as many argue—just a symptom of poverty or poor choices, but rather evidence of a new racial caste system at work.

(The New Jim Crow, p. 16).

W e live in a time of great paradox. Our nation has elected (and re-elected) its first black president, something that seemed a distant fantasy just a few decades ago. African Americans are no longer forced to use separate bathrooms, eat at separate lunch counters, or sit at the back of the bus. Jim Crow laws that authorized race discrimi-nation in employment, housing, and education have been struck down. Poll taxes and literacy tests that once operated to keep black people from voting have been abandoned.

Most people of all colors will say so much has changed in the United States. They'll say, just look at all the black lawyers, doctors, and athletic stars. Just look at Barack Obama, Oprah Winfrey, and Colin Powell. Our nation has come a long way. And then the familiar line, "but of course we still have a long way to go."

This kind of talk, this familiar line, implies that we're on the right path; that if we just keep plodding along, keep forging ahead, sooner or later we'll reach the Promised Land.

In 1968, after the major civil rights victories had been won, and the old Jim Crow had been brought to its knees, Martin Luther King Jr. warned that things are not always as they seem, and that a parallel universe continued to exist for poor people of color in the United States. He said:

> There are two Americas. One America is beautiful. In this America, millions of people have the milk of prosperity and the honey of equality flowing before them. This America is the habitat of millions of people who have food and material necessities for their bodies, culture and education for their minds, freedom and human dignity for their spirits. In this America children grow up in the sunlight of opportunity. But there is another America. This other America has a daily ugliness about it that transforms the buoyancy of hope into the fatigue of despair. (From "The Other America," March 14, 1968).

In the introduction to *The New Jim Crow*, Michelle Alexander acknowledges her own reluctance, because of her biases and assumptions, to accept the harsh realities that her experience and research came to teach her about race, drugs, and criminal justice in the United States. Even though she was an African American woman dedicated to racial and social justice, she had failed to see—she did not want to see—the "other America" that was hidden from her in plain sight. A new "caste system" had emerged, one that shuttles children in ghettoized communities from rundown, under-funded schools to brand new, high-tech prisons. A system that locks poor people—overwhelmingly poor people of color—into a permanent, second-class status eerily reminiscent of an era we supposedly left behind.

In chapter one, Alexander relates what she saw after the blinders—the long-held biases and assumptions—had fallen from her eyes. She starts by locating the rise of the system of mass incarceration within its historical context. Since our nation's founding, African Americans have repeatedly been controlled through white supremacist systems of racial and social control which appear to die, but are reborn in new form, tailored to the needs and constraints of the times. Time and again those who benefit from racial hierarchy have exploited our nation's racial divisions, stereotypes, and anxieties for political or economic gain—typically by pitting poor and working class whites against poor people of color. It seems that nothing is more threatening to the racial status quo than alliances that are formed across racial lines among poor and working class people. And nothing is more successful at destroying those alliances than introducing new caste systems aimed squarely at poor people of color, our society's chosen inhabitants of the "other America."

DISCUSSION TOPICS AND QUESTIONS:

1. Initial Reaction

When you first opened *The New Jim Crow*, what beliefs about race, racial progress, and our criminal justice system did you hold? Were you inclined to believe the claim that mass incarceration is "a new Jim Crow"? What biases, stereotypes, or assumptions might influence your thinking about the issues explored in this book? What life experiences have shaped your views?

2. Meaning of Caste

By describing the system of mass incarceration as a "caste" system, *The New Jim Crow* calls attention to the fact that millions of people labeled as "felons" or "criminals" are barred by law from mainstream society. As explained on page 13, "Like Jim Crow (and slavery), mass incarceration operates as a tightly networked system of laws, policies, customs and institutions that operate collectively to ensure the subordinate status of a group defined largely by race." Mass incarceration impacts not only those who are under the formal control of the criminal justice system (in prison or jail, on probation or parole), but also the tens of millions who are governed by laws authorizing legal discrimination against people released from prison. How do you feel about describing mass incarceration as a caste system? What might it mean for a nation to be home to a caste-like system while claiming democracy as its foundation?

3. *How Close to Home?*

Are you, or is anyone you know locked in the second-class status described here—unable to vote or legally discriminated against in employment, housing, education, or access to public benefits? What do you know, personally, about the struggles of those who are part of the undercaste?

4. *Movement Also Returns*

Chapter one's description of the re-emergence of caste in the United States is tethered to its description of what it has taken to bring past incarnations of caste (slavery and Jim Crow) to an end. The implication is that as caste re-emerges so too do social movements determined to end caste. As you ponder the existence of mass incarceration in the present-day United States, how does it feel to also consider that the ages-old movement for freedom and justice is also here among us? Do you feel a living connection to that old, yet new movement?

5. *Narrow Focus*

Although the book's thesis is sweeping in scope, many issues and groups of people are excluded from the analysis. From pages 15–16:

> This book paints with a broad brush, and as a result, many important issues have not received the attention they deserve. For example, relatively little is said here about the unique experience of women, Latinos, and immigrants in the criminal justice system, though those groups are particularly vulnerable to the worst abuses

and suffer in ways that are important and distinct. This book focuses on the experience of African American men in the new caste system. I hope other scholars and advocates will pick up where the book leaves off and develop the critique more fully or apply the themes sketched here to other groups and other contexts.

Women are the fastest growing segment of our nation's prison system, with the vast majority of the increase being impoverished African American and Latino women ensnared by the drug war. Latinos are the primary targets of the drug war in some states, and because of rampant immigration arrests, they now represent the majority population in U.S. federal prisons. The fastest growing segment of the private prison industry is private detention centers designed for people suspected of entering the country illegally. Youth of color are entering the juvenile justice system at alarming rates, largely due to what many describe as an inherently racist "School-to-Prison Pipeline." What is lost by excluding these groups and issues from the book's analysis? What might be gained by exploring, in depth, the impact of mass incarceration on one particular group? What people and perspectives are missing from your study circle?

6. *Racial Bribes*
In chapter one, the "divide and conquer" political tactics that helped to birth slavery, Jim Crow, and mass incarceration are explored in detail. Alexander argues that poor whites have repeatedly been offered "racial bribes." That is, special, largely superficial privileges

have been extended to poor whites in an effort to drive a wedge between them and poor blacks. Dr. King made a similar observation fifty years ago:

> The Southern aristocracy took the world and gave the poor white man Jim Crow. And when his wrinkled stomach cried out for the food that his empty pockets could not provide, he ate Jim Crow, a psychological bird that told him that no matter how bad off he was, at least he was a white man, better than a black man. (From "Address at the Conclusion of the Selma to Montgomery March," March 25, 1965).

When you read this chapter, was any of the history new to you? Do you see similar "divide and conquer" dynamics at work today? If so, what are they? Is the "get tough" movement aimed at those labeled "illegal immigrants" an example of racial bribes in action— i.e., promising to crack down on a racial or ethnic minority and deny them basic civil and human rights, while failing to improve the status of poor whites by much? What are the implications of these recurring tactics for the future of social justice organizing and advocacy? And, from another angle, do you see divide and conquer experiences developing *within* communities of color around issues of class?

7. *Is Beloved Community Possible?*

The book explains that as slavery in the United States ran its course, white supremacy came to resemble a kind of religion for the white community. On page 26, Alexander writes: "This deep faith in white supremacy not only justified an economic and political system in which plantation owners acquired land and great wealth through the brutality, torture, and coercion of other human beings; it also endured, like most articles of faith, long after the historical circumstances that gave rise to the religion passed away."

In the face of the history of white privilege and supremacy in the United States, the call for a movement to end our longstanding cycle of caste is incredibly bold. Some respected thinkers, such as Derrick Bell, seriously challenge that such a goal is achievable, contending that there is permanence to racism and racial hierarchy in the United States—that these tendencies are hard-wired into the fabric of our national life. Do you believe that Dr. King's vision of a beloved community can be realized in the United States? How do your feelings on this subject impact how you relate to the call to end mass incarceration and our nation's cycle of caste?

Photo © Julia Rendleman—juliarendleman.com

SECTION TWO:
HOW THE SYSTEM WORKS

(Chapters Two and Three)

A bit of common sense is overdue in public discussions
about racial bias in the criminal justice system. The
great debate over whether black men have been targeted
by the criminal justice system or unfairly treated in
the War on Drugs often overlooks the obvious. What
is painfully obvious when one steps back from indi-
vidual cases and specific policies is that the system of
mass incarceration operates with stunning efficiency to
sweep people of color off the streets, lock them in cages,
and then release them into an inferior second-class
status.

(*The New Jim Crow*, p. 103).

We now turn to the criminal justice system itself—
how it actually functions, as opposed to how it is
advertised. Chapters two and three are devoted to describing and debunking the myths that have rationalized and
sustained mass incarceration. These chapters demonstrate
how unchecked police authority, fiscal incentives, and a

Supreme Court that has disregarded basic civil rights have all facilitated the emergence of a legal caste system.

The legality of mass incarceration does not distinguish it from earlier systems of racial and social control. As Martin Luther King Jr. famously wrote in his "Letter from Birmingham Jail":

> We should never forget that everything Adolf Hitler did in Germany was "legal" and everything the Hungarian freedom fighters did in Hungary was "illegal." It was "illegal" to aid and comfort a Jew in Hitler's Germany. Even so, I am sure that, had I lived in Germany at the time, I would have aided and comforted my Jewish brothers.

It is not uncommon for people to say that when it comes to issues of racial justice, things are more complicated today than they were back in the days of the old Jim Crow. Back then, there were "whites only" signs, and everyone understood that black folks had to sit at the back of the bus. There was no denying the existence of a caste system. But today, things seem more complicated. Prisons are out of sight and out of mind. The "whites only" signs are gone, and nearly everyone denies racial bias. The justifications and rationalizations for mass incarceration seem more reasonable, because they are not explicitly based on race, and it is easy to imagine (especially if you are not directly affected) that nothing like an immoral caste system exists in the United States. It can be difficult to remember that not too long ago the old Jim Crow system was considered a sensible, rational response to a "complicated" situation in the South.

Dr. King's piercing honesty is instructive for us—how he refused to shrug off injustice when a given situation was deemed "complicated." In a sermon at the Temple of Israel in Hollywood in 1965, he insisted that "racial segregation must be seen for what it is—and that is an evil system, a new form of slavery covered up with certain niceties of complexity." Similarly, Dr. King steadfastly resisted efforts to assign words like "sensible" or "reasonable" to policies and attitudes that reflect a basic disregard for people's humanity. Like Dr. King, *The New Jim Crow* confronts our tendency to rationalize the suffering of others and the injustice that causes it. In these chapters, the book breaks through the veil of complexity that surrounds mass incarceration by exposing the principal myths that have been offered in its defense, including these:

- Surging incarceration rates can be explained by crime rates;
- Most people cycling in and out of the criminal justice system are violent offenders;
- People of color are more likely to use and sell illegal drugs than whites;
- The drug war has been focused on rooting out violent offenders and drug kingpins;
- Most people charged with crimes are provided with meaningful legal representation; and,
- The U.S. Constitution's guarantee of "equal protection under the law" protects racial minorities from bias in the criminal justice system.

None of the above myths are fact, yet their widespread acceptance has enabled our national community to deny or altogether ignore the truth about mass incarceration and its impacts across the United States.

DISCUSSION TOPICS AND QUESTIONS:

1. Main Myths

Many Americans are stunned to learn the facts about mass incarceration. Even in the hardest hit communities, people often blame themselves (or their children) for staggering arrest and incarceration rates. Many believe that mass incarceration is something that can be explained simply by "bad choices," but do not realize that kids on the other side of town are also using and selling drugs, and making other bad choices, without having to pay for such mistakes for the rest of their lives. Did you believe any of the main myths that rationalize mass incarceration before you read *The New Jim Crow*? To what extent is consciousness-raising about these myths necessary in order to create an environment in which people are willing to challenge misinformation and the status quo?

2. Mainstream Media

At the beginning of chapter two, Alexander states that the way the criminal justice system actually functions is vastly different from the way it is advertised in the mainstream media through shows like *Law and Order*. How does the mainstream media portray our criminal justice system? How are "criminals" depicted? What voices are most frequently heard in news coverage of crime? Whose voices are missing? What are the images, ideas, and messages that have most influenced your beliefs and attitude about our criminal justice system? What about the beliefs and attitude of the public at large?

3. License to Discriminate

Chapter three explains that the U.S. Supreme Court has made it virtually impossible to challenge racial bias in the courts at any stage of the criminal justice process, from stops and searches, to plea bargaining and sentencing. In some ways, this situation is reminiscent of *Plessy v. Ferguson*, which embraced the "separate but equal" doctrine and protected the old Jim Crow regime from legal challenge. What can be done to expose and challenge racial bias in the system if the Supreme Court won't address it? Can the strategies of earlier movements be a guide, or are new approaches necessary?

4. Police Power

The Supreme Court has eviscerated constitutional protections against unreasonable searches and seizures, effectively giving the police license to stop and search anyone, anywhere, at any time. Did you know the law had changed in this way? Have you ever been the victim of a stop and search by the police on the street or in your vehicle? How many times? What did it feel like? If you have never experienced it, why do you think that is?

5. Who Benefits from the War on Drugs?

Alexander notes that many law enforcement officials—including conservatives—were not eager to jump on board with the War on Drugs, because local communities were more concerned about serious crimes such as murder, rape, and robbery. The Reagan administration overcame this initial resistance by offering millions of dollars to state and local law enforcement agencies that would boost the sheer numbers of drug arrests. It became a numbers game driven by cash. Alexander writes: "Every system of control depends on the tangible and intangible benefits that are provided to those responsible for the system's maintenance and administration. This system is no exception," (*The New Jim Crow*, p. 72). What are some of the other benefits, besides cash, that this system provides to those who support it? Who benefits from the system as is, and who is harmed? Would changing the financial incentives be enough to end the system? Why or why not?

6. *Violence*

Relatively little is said in these chapters about violent crime. The focus is the War on Drugs. Alexander explains that, although half of state prisoners are violent offenders in some states, that statistic can be misinterpreted. Violent offenders typically receive much longer sentences than non-violent offenders, who receive shorter sentences but cycle in and out of the system. She emphasizes that what matters most is the prison label, not prison time. Of the nearly 7.3 million people under correctional control, 1.6 million are actually in prison. The rest are in jail or on probation or parole. More than 50 million people have been labeled criminals and felons and are subject to legal discrimination for the rest of their lives. Only a tiny percentage of these are violent offenders, yet this massive system is justified as a necessary means of dealing with people our society fears.

a) Do you believe that legitimate fears about violence play a larger role in public support for mass incarceration than is acknowledged here? Is it possible to build a movement to end mass incarceration in communities plagued by violent crime without offering solutions to the violence that threatens people's basic security?

b) Does focusing on the War on Drugs and non-violent offenders send the message that it is permissible to shame, dehumanize, and marginalize people so long as they're classified as violent? Should the movement to end mass incarceration offer hope of rehabilitation, redemption, and restoration to violent offenders as well as non-violent offenders?

c) In his book *When Work Disappears: The World of the New Urban Poor*, William Julius Wilson cites data that indicates when you compare white jobless men with black jobless men, racial disparities in violent crime disappear. Education and job creation are essential to safe, thriving communities. Locking up people en masse has proven to be an abysmal failure in dealing with violent crime rates. Cities like Chicago and New Orleans have the highest incarceration rates in the world yet are plagued by high levels of violent crime. Should the movement to end mass incarceration be linked to demands for quality education and jobs? Or is it important for the movement to have a sharper, narrower focus?

7. Diversity and Punitiveness

Research conducted by The Sentencing Project, an organization that advocates for alternatives to incarceration and promotes reforms in sentencing policy, shows that the countries that are the most racially and ethnically diverse are the most punitive, whereas the most homogeneous countries are the least punitive. Why do you think that is?

The United States is the most punitive country in the world. As described in chapter two, our nation imposes harsh mandatory minimum sentences on drug offenders—sentences sometimes harsher than murderers receive in other Western democracies. In fact, in the United States, there are people serving life sentences for first-time drug offenses, something that is unheard of anywhere else in the world. Although "diversity is our strength" is a nice-sounding slogan, the reality is that diversity may well be our nation's greatest challenge. As our nation witnesses the development of a new majority of people of color, and as demands for equality continue to be made, we see predictable backlashes and "get tough" demands against African Americans and other people of color, especially Latino immigrants. Could it be that building a movement to end mass incarceration—and thus transforming the punitive impulse into a compassionate one—is the ultimate test of whether the United States will ever achieve Dr. King's dream?

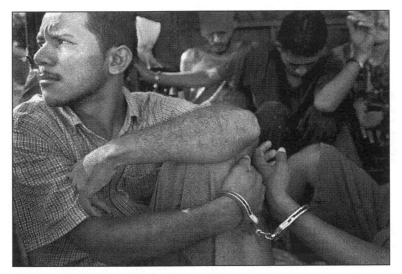

Photo © Jon Lowenstein—noorimages.com

SECTION THREE:
RACIAL INDIFFERENCE AND THE UNDERCASTE

(Chapters Four and Five)

Criminals, it turns out, are the one social group in America we have permission to hate. . . . Like the "coloreds" in the years following emancipation, criminals today are deemed a characterless and purposeless people, deserving of our collective scorn and contempt. When we say someone was "treated like a criminal," what we mean to say is that he or she was treated as less than human, like a shameful creature. Hundreds of years ago, our nation put those who were considered less than human in shackles; less than one hundred years ago, we relegated them to the other side of town; today we put them in cages. Once released, they find that a heavy and cruel hand has been laid upon them.

(*The New Jim Crow*, p. 141).

The system of mass incarceration has birthed a vast new undercaste—a permanent second-class status occupied by millions. In this section, we will explore the way that we as human beings find it disturbingly easy to treat others as disposable or unworthy of care and concern once they are labeled blameworthy or inferior in some fundamental respect. Once people are labeled in a way that makes them seem less like "us," a predictable set of beliefs, attitudes, policies, and practices begins to emerge.

These chapters of *The New Jim Crow* illustrate that overt racial hostility is not the most insidious attribute of this process of otherization. Racial indifference, the book contends, is the much more powerful foe facing us down. The immoral legal systems developed to govern those viewed as "less than" in our society only exist and endure because of the extreme racial indifference in our society. The War on Drugs and the system of mass incarceration not only reflect our collective racial anxieties and our tendency to treat the "other" as unworthy and disposable, they reflect a deep, very basic lack of care and attention. The absence of such care and attention makes awareness and change impossible.

Martin Luther King Jr. and his co-workers were obviously all too well acquainted with patterns of otherization and the insidious power of racial indifference. King's frustration with the "lukewarm acceptance" of "the white moderate" of his time bears this out with force:

> I have almost reached the regrettable conclusion that the Negro's great stumbling block in his stride toward freedom is not the White Citizens' Counciler or the Ku Klux Klanner, but the white moderate, who is more devoted to "order" than to justice; who prefers a negative peace which is the absence of tension to a positive peace which is the presence of justice; who constantly

says: "I agree with you in the goal you seek, but I cannot agree with your methods of direct action"; who paternalistically believes he can set the timetable for another man's freedom; who lives by a mythical concept of time and who constantly advises the Negro to wait for a "more convenient season." Shallow understanding from people of good will is more frustrating than absolute misunderstanding from people of ill will. Lukewarm acceptance is much more bewildering than outright rejection. (From "Letter from Birmingham Jail," 1963).

Black shame and complicity play a significant role in this process as well. As explained in these chapters, fear, self-hatred, and resignation lead many to remain silent about their suffering and to tolerate the severe injustice leveled at those consigned to our nation's undercaste. Such silence not only shores up the racial indifference in our society, it deadens the spirit of those trapped by it. As Dr. King once put it, "Our lives begin to end the day we become silent about things that matter."

King and his co-workers risked their lives to defeat the lie that some lives are worth more than others. Their struggle was rooted in the reclamation and assertion of personal dignity—the inestimable value of every human life, even the lives of our oppressors. Their movement was not merely a political or social struggle for civil rights; its core values were deeply moral and spiritual, urging us to move beyond blame, cruelty, self-interest, and division. We were called upon, and continue to be called upon, to choose the road less traveled—a path of forgiveness, compassion, service, and oneness.

DISCUSSION TOPICS AND QUESTIONS:

1. Dehumanization

Re-read the quotation from chapter four at the beginning of this section. What happens when we begin to view people as less than human, as shameful or characterless? Are there parallels to the treatment of those thought to be "illegal aliens"? Many of the same human rights—such as access to education, food, and work—are denied to people who have committed the "crime" of entering the country without proper documentation. What are the parallels between the "get tough" movement aimed at immigrants and the "get tough" laws aimed at African Americans?

2. Human Rights

Laws that authorize discrimination in employment, housing, education, and public benefits make it difficult, if not impossible, for people to find work in the legal economy, and greatly increase the likelihood that they will be arrested again. But are any of these laws necessary? Do you agree with Dr. King that everyone has basic human rights to work, food, education, and shelter? Should employers and housing officials ever have the right to discriminate against people with criminal records? Under some circumstances? In certain professions? For how long? Are community safety, human dignity, and racial justice advanced or undermined by the positions you take on these questions?

3. *Shame*

Chapter four discusses the shame and self-hatred that consumes a great many people labeled criminals and felons, and notes that "gangsta rap" is an expression of desperation—an attempt by young people to carve out a source of pride and make a statement of defiance to a society that despises them. What can we do to address the severe shame and self-hatred that keeps communities impacted by mass incarceration divided, often shaming and blaming each other? Are there sources of identity and pride that young people can embrace, even as they are targeted for incarceration and demonized by the larger society?

4. *White Privilege*

Re-read Martin Luther King's quotation pertaining to the "white moderate." Is it still true today that whites prefer "order" to justice? What can be done to bring about a fuller acknowledgement of white privilege in our society and its far-reaching, often devastating consequences? What can be done to cultivate more concern, understanding, and cooperation across racial lines?

5. *Human Failings*

Michelle Alexander has stated that ending the stigma and shame heaped on people with criminal records requires all of us—including those of us who have not been to prison—to acknowledge our own criminality, sins, mistakes, and failings. After all, we are all flawed, and we have all likely broken the law at some point in our lives. Falling down and making mistakes is part of what makes us human. The U.S. criminal justice system depends upon us ignoring our own sins and mistakes while condemning the sins and mistakes of others. In many other countries, going to jail does not mean you are a bad person, but simply a person who once did a bad thing. Do you agree that in order to end mass incarceration, a cultural shift of this kind is needed?

6. *Collateral Damage*

Chapter five explores a number of differences between mass incarceration and earlier systems of racial and social control. Some of the differences, Alexander points out, are not necessarily as big as they appear. Others are significant. One of the most obvious differences is that mass incarceration directly harms far more white people than Jim Crow. Some people imagine that Jim Crow harmed only African Americans, but Dr. King repeatedly emphasized that it hurt white people too—particularly poor whites. He explained:

> The moral justification for special measures for Negroes is rooted in the robberies inherent in the institution of slavery. Many poor whites, however, were the derivative victims of slavery. As long as labor was cheapened by the involuntary servitude of the black man, the freedom of white labor, especially in the South, was little more than a myth. It was free only to bargain from the depressed base imposed by slavery upon the whole labor market. Nor did this derivative bondage end when formal slavery gave way to the de-facto slavery of dis-

crimination. To this day the white poor also suffer de-
privation and the humiliation of poverty if not of color.
They are chained by the weight of discrimination,
though its badge of degradation does not mark them. It
corrupts their lives, frustrates their opportunities and
withers their education. In one sense it is more evil for
them, because it has confused so many by prejudice that
they have supported their own oppressors. (From *Why
We Can't Wait*, 1964).

In chapter five, Alexander states that white people
are "collateral damage" in the War on Drugs—not
the original target, but harmed nonetheless. Do you
agree? Who else is harmed by the drug war but might
nevertheless believe it is in their interests? Borrowing
again from Dr. King's "Letter from Birmingham Jail,"
how can we help awaken people of all colors to the reality that we are "caught in an inescapable network of
mutuality, tied in a single garment of destiny"? Do you
agree with King that "whatever affects one directly, affects all"?

7. Racial Indifference

Many would argue that mass incarceration is different
from Jim Crow because of the lack of overt racial hostility. Alexander acknowledges that, unlike the days of
Jim Crow, few people today are proud to call themselves racist. On page 203, she writes: "Things have
changed . . . [and] this difference in public attitudes
has important implications for reform efforts." But
on the whole, Alexander maintains that mass incarceration depends far more on racial indifference than

racial hostility. Do you agree that mass incarceration is rooted in racial indifference—a lack of care and concern across lines of race and class? If so, how do we inspire greater compassion and care? Research suggests that people interpret and understand the world through stories. Do the stories of those trapped in the system need to be told and heard? What else can be done?

8. *A New Underground Railroad*
In numerous speeches, Alexander has argued that we should commit ourselves to building an "underground railroad" for people returning home from prison. Movement building, she argues, requires working for the abolition of the system of mass incarceration as a whole, as well as providing desperately needed support and love to people at risk of incarceration, families with loved ones behind bars, and people returning home from prison. The movement must acknowledge and respond to the human suffering caused by this system and model what a compassionate society actually looks like. Do you agree? If so, what can we do, individually and collectively, to offer greater support, resources, and love to people struggling to survive the system of mass incarceration?

Photo © Lloyd DeGrane—lloyddegrane.com

SECTION FOUR:
THE MOVEMENT

(Chapter Six)

If Martin Luther King Jr. is right that the arc of the
moral universe is long, but it bends toward justice, a new
movement will arise; and if civil rights organizations
fail to keep up with the times, they will be pushed to
the side as another generation of advocates comes to
the fore. Hopefully the new generation will be led by
those who know best the brutality of the new caste
system—a group with greater vision, courage, and
determination than the old guard can muster, trapped
as they may be in an outdated paradigm. This new
generation of activists should not disrespect their elders
or disparage their contributions or achievements; to
the contrary, they should bow their heads in respect,
for their forerunners have expended untold hours and
made great sacrifices in an elusive quest for justice. But
once respects have been paid, they should march right
past them, emboldened, as King once said, by the fierce
urgency of now.

(*The New Jim Crow*, p. 260).

Keeping company with the final chapter of *The New Jim Crow*, this section is devoted to the question of where we go from here. Michelle Alexander argues that we, as a nation, have reached a fork in the road. Likewise, here at the end of our journey with her book, we find ourselves at a critical point of decision. What is required of us at this moment in history, a time when millions are cycling in and out of our nation's prisons and jails—trapped in a parallel social universe in which discrimination is perfectly legal? How do we show care and concern for the children who are born into communities where the majority of men and growing numbers of women can expect to spend time behind bars? What must we do, now that we know that the usual justifications do not hold water, and that a human rights nightmare is occurring on our watch?

The New Jim Crow begins and ends with the assertion that nothing short of a major social movement holds any hope of ending mass incarceration in the United States. If we were to return to the rates of incarceration we had in the 1970s—before the drug war and get tough movement gained steam—we would have to release four out of five people who are in prison today. More than a million people employed by the criminal justice system would lose their jobs. Private prison companies listed on the New York Stock Exchange would be forced to watch their profits vanish. This system has become so deeply rooted in our political, social, and economic structure that mere "tinkering with the machine" has no hope of bringing it down. While piecemeal policy reform efforts and colorblind cost-benefit approaches may seem pragmatic in the short run, they leave intact the racial attitudes, stereotypes, and anxieties that gave rise to the system in the first place. As long as poor people of color are viewed as largely disposable, with the primary limiting principle being how much it costs to throw them away, caste-like systems will be a recurring, if not permanent, feature of American life.

Martin Luther King Jr. knew what it felt like to face what seemed to be an impassable barrier. And in such situations he understood all too well the tension between what appears politically feasible and what is morally right and necessary. As he observed:

> Cowardice asks the question, "Is it safe?" Expediency asks the question, "Is it politic?" And Vanity comes along and asks the question, "Is it popular?" But Conscience asks the question, "Is it right?" And there comes a time when one must take a position that is neither safe, nor politic, nor popular, but he must do it because Conscience tells him it is right. (From "A Proper Sense of Priorities," February 6, 1968).

In the face of mass incarceration and in light of *The New Jim Crow*'s call to action, what do we hear the voice of Conscience saying to us now, at this time, in this place?

DISCUSSION TOPICS AND QUESTIONS:

1. Reform or Transform?

In chapter six, Alexander argues that "tinkering with the machine" will not be enough to end the cycle of caste in the United States. On page 259, arguing for what Dr. King described as a "radical restructuring of society," she cites one of his most powerful addresses to the Southern Christian Leadership Conference (SCLC):

> A human rights movement, King believed, held revolutionary potential. . . . In May 1967, he told SCLC staff . . . "It is necessary for us to realize that we have moved from the era of civil rights to the era of human rights. . . . After Selma and the voting rights bill, we moved into [this] new era, which must be an era of revolution. We must see the great distinction between a reform movement and a revolutionary movement. We are called upon to raise certain basic questions about the whole society." (From "To Chart Our Course for the Future," May 22, 1967).

Do you agree with the distinction Alexander makes between isolated, piecemeal policy reform efforts and building a movement in which truly transformational change is possible? Aside from the civil rights movement, are there other movements that might offer guidance, models, or inspiration for what we aim to achieve?

2. A New Moral Consensus
In *Where Do We Go from Here* (1967), Martin Luther King Jr. wrote:

> Let us not be misled by those who argue that segregation cannot be ended by the force of law. But acknowledging this, we must admit that the ultimate solution to the race problem lies in the willingness of men to obey the unenforceable. Court orders and federal enforcement agencies are of inestimable value in achieving desegregation,

but desegregation is only a partial, though necessary step toward the final goal which we seek to realize, genuine intergroup and interpersonal living. Desegregation will break down the legal barriers and bring men together physically, but something must touch the hearts and souls of men so that they will come together spiritually because it is natural and right. A vigorous enforcement of civil rights laws will bring an end to segregated public facilities which are barriers to a truly desegregated society, but it cannot bring an end to fears, prejudice, pride, and irrationality, which are the barriers to a truly integrated society. Those dark and demonic responses will be removed only as men are possessed by the invisible, inner law which etches on their hearts the conviction that all men are brothers and love is mankind's most potent weapon for personal and social transformation. True integration will be achieved by true neighbors who are willingly obedient to unenforceable obligations.

Embedded in *The New Jim Crow*'s call for a broad-based, human rights movement on behalf of poor people of all colors is the call for the forging of a "new moral consensus." What moral consensus, what "unenforceable obligations," do you think ought to be at the heart of the movement to end mass incarceration and the cycle of caste in the United States? What core values and commitments should drive the movement's work and exemplify its character?

3. First Steps

Dr. King once urged advocates not to be afraid if they were unable to draft a clear road map for bringing about change. He said you don't need to see the whole staircase in order to take the first step. What do you believe are the first steps? What specific actions can we take, individually or collectively, in our schools, places of worship, communities, etc., to engage in movement building? Do we need to create new organizations and coalitions, or are the existing organizations adequate to the tasks that lie ahead?

4. *Areas of Work*

In her speeches, Alexander identifies three, interrelated, equally important areas of work: 1) consciousness-raising so that an awakening within communities of all colors can begin; 2) building an "underground railroad" that will provide support to all those directly impacted by the system; and 3) organizing for abolition of the system of mass incarceration as a whole, including advocacy to end the drug war, to end discrimination against people branded criminals, and to shift from a purely punitive approach to dealing with violence and violent crime to a more rehabilitative and restorative one. Do you agree with these priorities? What areas of work are missing from this list?

5. *Who's at the Table?*

History suggests that it is crucial to the success of social movements that the people on whose behalf the movement speaks and acts need to themselves have a seat at the table when movement decisions are made and the character and culture of the movement is developed. Are prisoners and former prisoners finding a seat at the table in this movement? Why or why not?

Do you think a new underground railroad could help make it possible for formerly incarcerated people to find their way to a seat at the table? And where is this table anyway? Shouldn't prisoners and former prisoners be hosts rather than guests at the movement's organizing table?

6. *Colorblindness*
Throughout *The New Jim Crow,* "colorblindness" is described as the belief that not seeing race, or seeing beyond race, represents a virtuous social goal. The book argues that colorblindness is not only a shortsighted belief, but that it has been routinely used as a manipulative tool to advance drug war/mass incarceration policies. How do you respond to the book's depiction of colorblindness? Do you see redeeming qualities in the concept of seeing beyond race? Do you agree with Alexander's conclusion that dealing openly with race is essential to the struggle at hand, and that the goal of colorblindness should be abandoned?

7. *Affirmative Action*
In chapter six, Alexander suggests that affirmative action may be operating more like a racial bribe than a tool for transformative change. She argues that affirmative action embraces a "trickle down theory of racial justice," offers "cosmetic diversity" without genuine equality, creates the appearance of racial progress without the reality, and pits poor and working people against each other, fighting for scraps, rather than working together for justice. How do you respond to this critique? Has Alexander's analysis of affirmative

action impacted your own views? How do you think the complex issue of affirmative action comes to bear on the work of movement building?

8. *International Dimension*
Recalling section one's discussion of those issues and groups excluded from the book's analysis, as we consider the building up of a movement to end mass incarceration, which necessitates ending the War on Drugs, let us consider the international nature of the struggle. To what extent is the movement we are attempting to build linked to movements in other countries? Unspeakable suffering is occurring, for example, across the border in Mexico, where the War on Drugs has become a very literal war. Between 2006 and 2012 more than sixty thousand people were killed and twenty thousand were disappeared in Mexico. As with modern warfare in general, the vast majority of these drug war victims were unarmed civilians. Most of the weapons used to inflict the continuing, brutal violence in Mexico flows north-to-south from the United States. Meanwhile, the overwhelming demand for drugs in the United States creates the enormous cash-flow that fuels the constant south-to-north flow of drugs from Mexico, which leaves this horrific violence and death in its wake. Isn't the struggle to end mass incarceration in the United States connected to the struggle and suffering of our brothers and sisters in Mexico and elsewhere throughout the world? Should we make it a movement priority to demonstrate solidarity with people engaged in similar struggles around the world? What might that look like?

9. Commitment and Sacrifice

Do you think that building this movement will demand the same level of sacrifice as the struggle for freedom called forth during the civil rights era? For what level of sacrifice do you feel prepared? What would help to prepare you for this work? Are you part of a community that is knit tightly enough to support you and/or join you in a serious consideration of bold action? If not, what steps can you take to create or locate yourself in such a community? Or, what steps can you take to persuade the community of which you're already a part to move into a place, spiritually and practically, to embrace more radical, truly transformational steps? What are you willing to do now?

Made in the USA
Lexington, KY
21 November 2016